THE ISRAEL MISSION LEADER'S GUIDE

To

ISRAEL—A Spiritual Travel Guide, 2nd Edition

A Companion for the Modern Jewish Pilgrim
by Rabbi Lawrence A. Hoffman

This guide was prepared with the assistance of
Rabbi Elliott Kleinman

JEWISH LIGHTS Publishing

A tour guide friend likes to say that he walks in the footsteps of Moses. After all, Moses was more than simply the leader of the Jewish people; he was also their tour leader. Imagine the task before him. Moses was responsible for dealing with the day-to-day problems of travel: making sure the people stayed together, that they had a place to stay each night and that they arrived at their destination. More than that, however, Moses was also the spiritual guide for the Jewish people. Not only was it his responsibility to bring their bodies to the Land of Israel; he was charged with the task of bringing their hearts and minds on a sacred pilgrimage.

The modern tour leader on a trip to Israel carries many of the same responsibilities and some of the same problems (issues with food, itinerary, accommodations, and such). More important, you are also responsible for guiding the hearts and hopes of the tour participants. Shimon Ovitz once said, "From each Jewish heart an invisible path leads to the Land of Israel." While that may be true, helping people's hearts find that path is your challenge.

A tour guide points out sights to be seen, a pilgrimage leader brings people to sites to be experienced. The work of leading a trip to Israel is sacred work. As a group leader you have an obligation to see not only to the physical needs of the participants but to enhance their spiritual encounter with the Land of Israel.

This guide will assist you in transforming ordinary trips into spiritual pilgrimages. In addition to some thoughts as to how best *Israel: A Spiritual Travel Guide* can be used with your group, this guide includes an additional section on visiting the grave of Yitzhak Rabin (on Mt. Herzl) and/or Kikar Rabin (Rabin Square in Tel Aviv). Finally, there is a place to keep important names and phone numbers.

How to Prepare
1. KNOW THE GROUP: COLLECT INFORMATION IN ADVANCE
Before you leave, get to know as much as possible about the group you are leading. Ask for lots of information as part of the

application/registration process. What do participants hope will happen on the trip? What will count as "success" when they return home? In what ways do they expect to be changed? Who has been to Israel before? Have good friends or family members been to Israel? Why are people choosing to go on this trip, and why now?

2. KNOW YOURSELF: WHAT ARE YOUR GOALS?
Determine your own goals for the group. Is it your desire that the trip affect individuals or the nature of the group or both? What do you want people to know when they return? What do you hope they will do, or do differently, when they return? How do you think/hope your relationship with the group and the individuals will evolve because of this trip? This information will help to design the trip curriculum that is most appropriate for you and the group. Visiting Israel is an educational, emotional and spiritual experience. Good experiences take good planning. Taking the time to ask the right questions will make planning the trip much easier.

3. ASSEMBLE THE GROUP IN ADVANCE
Essential to any group experience is the opportunity to build community together, to become a unit that works, learns and grows through shared experience. If at all possible, begin the process before you leave on your trip. Make a time for your group to get to know one another in an informal setting at least once before the trip. In the invitation to the first pre-travel session, consider including Reading 1 (pp. 18–19) from *Israel: A Spiritual Travel Guide*. At this first meeting, distribute copies of the book to each member (or family) in the group. It serves as both a guidebook and textbook for the pilgrimage to Israel. Most important, the book establishes shared expectations. In just a few minutes a day, people will more and more look forward to a particularly exciting trip, and will arrive in Israel fully ready to participate.

To start the meeting, ask people to introduce themselves and invite each person to voice their excitement and expectations, hopes and dreams about the upcoming trip. Then divide the group into two sections. Ask section one to read Readings 6 and 7 (pp. 27–30). Within the small group consider the following questions:

- In what ways do I think like a tourist and in what ways do I think like a pilgrim?
- What changes do I need to make in my expectations to become a better pilgrim?
- How might a pilgrimage affect me differently than a tour?

Ask the second small group to read Readings 8 and 9 (pp. 31–34). Within the small group consider the following questions:

- In what ways is Israel my home?
- In the past when I have traveled, what did I miss about my home?
- How do these feelings affect my pilgrimage to Israel?
- How will I know when I am "home" in Israel?

Bring the groups together and collect the responses on a blackboard or flip chart. Are there any surprises? In this short meeting the group has, for the first time, acted together to share individual feelings. This group commitment to the individual and the experience is an important building block for the trip.

If a second meeting is possible, ask participants to read Readings 10–14 (pp. 35–46) in advance. Put a large map of Israel on the wall for easy reference. Using what they have learned about the geography and history of Israel in those readings, go over the details of where the group will be traveling. Invite people to speculate about what different sites will mean to them. Acknowledge that everyone is already preparing for the trip—some are buying clothes or luggage, others are making arrangements for vacation from work or school. In what ways are they already preparing themselves spiritually? What are some additional ways to prepare spiritually for this pilgrimage? Spiritual preparation might include studying some of the sites to be visited, reading (or rereading) the introduction in *Israel: A Spiritual Travel Guide*, and/or beginning a personal journal of the pilgrimage.

Keeping a "Pilgrimage" Journal

If people have not read through all 18 of the preparatory readings, suggest that they do so. The readings are short but very moving. Show people the rituals for leaving home that are celebrated around the Shabbat table (p. 57) and in synagogue (p. 58), and invite participants to take part in them by inviting friends and family to dinner and by speaking to the rabbi and requesting a departing blessing at synagogue services.

People who participate in these opportunities for blessing report being exceptionally moved. They are more apt to find their entire journey more stimulating because they learn early to relate to Israel personally—as if this journey is somehow different; it is a journey of their own personal growth.

Leaders of trips to Israel have often found it helpful to provide participants with a journal book for the trip. That is why *Israel: A Spiritual Travel Guide* contains many empty pages for people to use to keep track of their thoughts and experiences. People should not feel that they have to write about each experience but they should feel free to use the journal at will and as they want—doodle, write, react, contemplate, keep a log of visits or a diary of feelings. Most significant is that time is taken to consider and reflect on each day's activities. Reading 18 (p. 53) suggests that journaling makes a wonderful gift to posterity. People who write nothing for themselves may be moved to reword their thoughts for children or grandchildren back home. They will thank you for suggesting it to them.

The Journey and Arrival in Israel

All too often we allow people to simply be passive absorbers of information. For this journey to become a pilgrimage, each participant must be fully involved. In your preparation for the journey, pay special attention to Section Three (pp. 61–79) of *Israel: A Spiritual Travel Guide*. As you gather at the airport, set the stage for a sacred pilgrimage by claiming a sacred moment amidst the hustle and bustle of the airport. Gather the group before boarding and recall with them the moment when God called to Abram and said, "Go forth from your native land, from the house of your ancestors and journey to the land that I will show you" (Genesis 12:1). Now as a group, you too will journey to the land to which God has directed the hearts and hands of Jews for generations. Acknowledge this great moment with the blessing on the bottom of page 74.

The excitement of departure notwithstanding, when groups get onto an airplane they quickly become individuals again, separated by seats, sleep and anticipation. Try doing things on the plane to keep the group focused. Upon request, travel agents will try to seat groups together. Take advantage of this opportunity. This is a great time to ask people to create their first journal entries.

As arrival time nears, but before the "fasten seat belt" light is illuminated, draw the group together again (either physically or by drawing their attention to you). Ask them to read the Prayer for Arrival on pages 75–76.

Airports are busy places. Arriving at the airport in Israel is confusing. Before people separate to gather their luggage, help them re-focus their hearts and minds on the spiritual, by gathering in a circle and reciting the blessing on page 76. Finally, once you board your bus, welcome people home and invite the group to consider aloud how arriving in Israel differed from arriving at other travel destinations.

If you are traveling to Jerusalem, use the blessings and readings on pages 77–79 as described. If your first night is not in Jerusalem, recite the *shehecheyanu* (p. 78) together on the bus as you travel to your first destination. After check-in, but before the group separates for the night, call a brief meeting.

These past hours have given people an opportunity to voice their feelings upon having set foot in the land of Israel. What surprised them? What do they look forward to tomorrow? Before people disperse for sleep, invite them to say together the prayer for retiring for the first night in Israel (p. 78).

Being a Pilgrim and a Pilgrimage Leader

Israel: A Spiritual Travel Guide offers a rich variety of readings and blessings for many of the sites you'll be visiting. Invest some time before the trip thinking about how you want to use them. Each day offers tour leaders a variety of challenges and opportunities. Much of your time will, of necessity, be devoted to assuring that the group gets to each destination, that people are not left behind and that you keep on schedule. It is very easy to let that work consume all of your time and attention. Try not to let that happen! Use this guide to help you focus your attention on being a pilgrimage leader. Israel is the place where heaven and earth touch. Take time to point out those connections.

Rabbi Hoffman suggests a wonderful way to encounter each site in Israel—anticipate, approach, acknowledge and reflect (he calls it "afterthought"). Using these concepts as a guide, you can assist members of the group to create their own link between heaven and earth.

Anticipation

The same tour guide friend I mentioned earlier notes that in the tour business, preparation is everything. This is no less true when on a pilgrimage. Spiritual preparation requires focus and information. Use additional readings, your comments, and those of the tour guide to ensure that people know enough about each site so they can fully appreciate its impact. Be sure they are spiritually prepared for that moment as well.

Israel: A Spiritual Travel Guide accomplishes this, but you should share your own feelings about particular moments or places that have touched or moved you. Invite your guide and/or bus driver to do the same. *There is nothing like the power of stories.* How do they feel at this place? What do they remember from the time they first visited here? These kinds of conversations go much deeper than historical data to connect people with the experience of being in Israel. They give participants a genuinely human glimpse of the potential each visit holds.

Sometimes, this will require that you offer information and/or opening thoughts the night before visiting a particular site. At other times, the bus ride to the site will provide that opportunity. Time spent on the bus need not be down time for people. Certainly people need a chance to relax and visit with each other, so be sure to give them "snooze and schmooze" time. Yet the bus also offers the wonder of relative seclusion from the hustle and bustle of the world. This kind of quiet is rare—make good use of it! Try using the anticipation readings as you ride to the site. Ask different people to read the passages aloud. Invite others to share what they are looking forward to, now that they have heard the passage.

Finally, keep in mind that speech and silence each have a power all their own. Certain visits may best be prepared for with introspective silence. The human voice, yours or anyone's, can become an intrusion into the private and sacred. For example, Yad Vashem is often a very personal moment and requires a certain sense of isolation to be fully appreciated. On the other hand, some experiences — like Masada — need the support and involvement of the entire group. Consider whether silence or sharing will best support a vivid and personal encounter with the spirit that is Israel.

Approach

Invariably there will be moments when the "approach" passage is best used after you have arrived at the site itself. Yet, there may also be moments when, for a variety of reasons, this passage is best used either on the bus or as you actually walk toward a particular site. When deciding, consider the site and the group. Should the group approach this site together or as individuals? Does the particular passage best lend itself to the quiet of the bus or would it be enhanced by the visual stimuli of the site? Is there space and opportunity to bring the group together at the site? Can you or someone else be heard at the site? One final note: *Just before you leave the bus, tell people what will happen and what you will be doing. If something is going to happen as a group, let the participants know what, when and where. People need above all to feel safe. They should never be in doubt about what is happening, and never suffer surprises.* Give people time to explore, but always tell them when, where and why the group will next gather.

Acknowledgment

The high point of *Israel: A Spiritual Travel Guide* is the acknowledgment section — usually a traditional blessing or reading that acknowledges the spiritual impact of the place being visited. Rabbi Hoffman suggests that each individual say the acknowledgment prayer at the moment of coming into face-to-face recognition of the power of each place. In each case he suggests where that might be.

You can help people acknowledge their experience by drawing people's attention in advance to the page number and place in question, so they will know what to do and where to do it. The endnotes (pp. 237–243) often supply the place where the blessing comes from. People sometimes like to know they will be citing the Talmud or a medieval pilgrimage manual. Give them this information in advance if you think it helpful.

Note that not everyone will say the acknowledgment then. A person often is best able to acknowledge a gift, friendship or moment after the gift has been received, the friendship tested or the moment experienced. With that in mind, people may want to experience each site fully before acknowledging it. So before you leave or move onto something else, give people the time to acknowledge that they are leaving, if they have not already done so. Many of the acknowledgments are wonderful catalysts also for the development of your own prayers or blessings. There may be times when members of the group will want to offer their own prayer or blessing for a special moment. If you offer people that option you will be pleasantly surprised how often and how well people will take advantage of the opportunity.

Reflection—Writing the Thought After

Research teaches us that experiences are best remembered when there is a conscious effort to place them into our memory to be recalled later. Remembering is not easy. Pictures are only representations of what happened. Feelings, thoughts and prayers are the substance of experience. Before every trip to Israel I purchase one of those books filled with blank pages and pledge to fill the pages with that substance at the end of each day. Unfortunately, time, events and forgetfulness conspire each time to keep too many of those pages empty. While you can't require people to write their experiences, you can remind them to do so. Moreover, you can provide time and a place to do so. This may be on the bus at the end of the day or following dinner in a hotel. Regardless, your active support for this process will, in the long run, be appreciated.

To help people focus their thoughts and feelings, ask some open-ended, leading or summary questions throughout the day (pp. 61–79 offer some ideas that may be helpful). Make sure that journaling is not an unnecessary burden. Provide pens and pencils, even extra journal books if the blank pages of *Israel: A Spiritual Travel Guide* are insufficient. On the other hand, the pages supplied may be enough, and using them allows participants to feel satisfied that they have "filled up the book" rather than made random notes in an arbitrary notebook somewhere.

Different Groups Require Different Strategies

ADULT FIRST-TIME VISITORS

In many ways, adults visiting Israel for the first time are the easiest groups with whom you can travel because they are relatively self-sufficient. They do, however, require plenty of attention to their spiritual needs as these can easily be subsumed by their regular tourist impulses. By asking people to share in reading aloud, asking questions, even leading prayers you help focus their attention on their role as spiritual pilgrims. *Israel: A Spiritual Travel Guide* provides everything necessary — transliterations, readings, everything. This is a *truly* "user-friendly" book. It requires no prior knowledge. Help people find their way comfortably within it.

ADULT REPEAT VISITORS

Frequent tourists can easily become blasé about places and even experiences encountered in their travels. Return visitors to Israel are different. Inside each of them is a set of experiences and information from past visits that can improve each subsequent visit. As the tour leader, you can unlock that information by inviting the participants to be partners with you in making this pilgrimage. Ask each participant or couple to prepare a favorite reading or personal comment for a particular site to supplement the passages in *Israel: A Spiritual Travel Guide*. Allow them to be the leaders of their own spiritual pilgrimage by bringing something from their own experiences to the rest of the group.

FAMILIES

My father used to say that there was no such thing as a family vacation, only family trips. The upshot of this philosophical nugget is that traveling with families adds both stress and potential to any trip. Make the most of family time. You may want to ask children to participate at special times, thus including them in leading the trip. Bar/bat mitzvah students make excellent candidates for this. As part of their preparation for the trip, assign them a place or event for which they will be asked to make a presentation. This assignment will give them, or anyone, more personal ownership of the trip. They should research and write about the place/event. When you reach that site or moment, the young person in your group can make their presentation.

Find ways to strengthen family interaction on your trip. Instead of reading passages or prayers as a group, find times and places when families can venture off on their own and, using *Israel: A Spiritual Travel Guide*, create their own family Israel experience. These experiences can be as simple as reading together what is in the book or sharing their innermost thoughts at the moment. Suggest that families find a place where they can be apart from the rest of your group and other people at the site. Read the passage(s) in the book. Each family member can then share what this site means to them, talk about what it must have been like to see it built, and imagine how others have encountered it through the years or what it might have meant to other Jews in other lands and other generations.

HIGH SCHOOL GROUPS

While students are the most receptive group to the potential of an Israel experience, students seem to specialize in distraction. *Israel: A Spiritual Travel Guide* can serve to focus and organize the students with whom you are traveling. Young people can be focused and empowered by holding their own book in their hands. Being responsible for making a presentation before, during or after certain events or places (as described in the section about adult repeat visitors) can help to more fully immerse them in the Israel experience.

Enhance the Experience—Don't Overprogram

Obviously we, as tour leaders, care deeply about the experience people have on trips we lead. *Israel: A Spiritual Travel Guide* is a wonderful tool to help make that pilgrimage experience as complete as possible. Yet, the book will not help you if you don't have it with you. Make sure you have your copy each day. *And make sure everyone on the trip has one too. Don't share books.* Everyone needs his or her own, since everyone is having his or her own experience. Remind participants each day to carry their copy with them. Take time to plan how, when and where you are going to use the book for that day. Finally, don't overuse the book or over-program people's spirits. Each group has a natural flow. Allow the group to set its own spiritual pace.

To be a part of YisraEl is to struggle with your own spiritual identity and to appreciate the value of the struggle. The Land and the People are inextricably bound together. A trip to Israel is a chance to encounter the land and discover what binds us as a Jewish people. Anticipate the wonders that await you and your group on this trip. Approach each day and each site as an opportunity. Acknowledge the moments of challenge and change that will inevitably occur. Reflect on your role and what leading a spiritual pilgrimage means to you.

A Prayer for Leaders on a Spiritual Pilgrimage to Israel

Sovereign of the universe, in awe I come before You, aware of the responsibility and opportunity that is mine, as I prepare to bring Your people Israel to their Land of Israel. Let this be a journey of insight and discovery. May we all find ourselves nearer to You with each step we take. Grant me strength of purpose, strength of spirit and strength of body that I, together with all those traveling with me, may find You, each other and ourselves in the Land of Israel.

On Visiting Rabin Square or the Grave of Yitzhak Rabin

ANTICIPATION

Yitzhak Rabin was born in Jerusalem on March 1, 1922. Inducted into the Haganah by Moshe Dayan, he was appointed deputy commander of the Palmach. In the spring of 1948 he commanded the Harel Brigade, leading it in Operation Nachshon to open the road to besieged Jerusalem, and liberating the city. Rabin became the seventh IDF Chief of Staff on January 1, 1964. As Chief of Staff, Rabin led the IDF to victory in the Six Day War. He retired from the army on January 1, 1968, and was named ambassador to the United States, where he served for five years.

In the spring of 1973, Rabin returned to Israel and became active in the Labor Party. He was elected Member of the Knesset in December 1973, and when Golda Meir formed her government in April 1974, was appointed Minister of Labor. Following the resignation of Golda Meir, on June 2, 1974, the Knesset expressed confidence in a new government headed by Prime Minister Yitzhak Rabin. He resigned from the premiership in April 1977.

Rabin was elected chairman of the Israel Labor Party in its first nationwide primaries conducted in February 1992, and led the party to victory in the June 1992 Knesset elections. In July 1992, Rabin formed Israel's 25th Government as Prime Minister and Minister of Defense.

Yitzhak Rabin was awarded the Nobel Prize for Peace in December 1994, along with Foreign Minister Shimon Peres and PLO Chairman Yasser Arafat.

APPROACH

Prime Minister Yitzhak Rabin's Address at Israeli-Palestinian Interim Agreement Signing Ceremony, Washington, D.C. September 28, 1995

I want to say to you, Chairman Arafat, the leader of the Palestinians: Together, we should not let the land flowing with milk and honey become a land flowing with blood and tears. Don't let it happen. If all the partners to the peace-making do not unite against the evil angels of death by terrorism, all that will remain of this ceremony are color snapshots, empty mementos. Rivers of hatred will overflow again — and swamp the Middle East. We, gentlemen, will not permit terrorism to defeat peace. We will not allow it. If we do not have partners in this bitter, difficult war, we will fight it alone. We know how to fight, and we know how to win.

My brother Jews: Thousands of years of exile and the dream of generations have returned us to our historic home in the Land of Israel, the Land of the Prophets.

Etched on every vineyard, every field, every olive tree, every flower is the deep imprint of Jewish history, of the Book of Books that we have bequeathed to the entire world, of the values of morality and justice.

Every place in the Land of the Prophets, every name is an integral part of our heritage of thousands of years, of the Divine promise to us and to our descendants. Here is where we were born. Here is where we created a nation. Here we forged a haven for the persecuted and built a model democratic country.

But we are not alone here on this soil, in this land. And so we are sharing this good earth today with the Palestinian people — in order to choose life. Starting today, an agreement on paper will be translated into reality on the ground.

ACKNOWLEDGMENT

Barukh atah Adonai Eloheinu melekh ha'olam shenatan mik'vodo l'vasar v'dam.

You abound in blessings, Eternal One our God, Sovereign of the universe, who has bestowed of Your dignity to human beings.

Important Information

Tour Company: _____

    Phone Number: _____

Bus Driver: _____

    Phone Number: _____

Guide: _____

    Phone Number: _____

Hotel: _____

    Phone Number: _____

Hotel: _____

    Phone Number: _____

Hotel: _____

    Phone Number: _____

Hotel: _____

    Phone Number: _____

Airline: _____

    Phone Number: _____

Air Travel Times: _____

_____

_____

_____

_____

_____

Other: _____

_____

_____

_____

_____

Printed in the USA
CPSIA information can be obtained
at www.ICGtesting.com
JSHW011416160824
R13664500002B/R136645PG68134JSX00027B/5